CLASSICAL LIVING

January 2006
ISBN: 907721352X

PUBLISHER

BETA-PLUS Publishing

Termuninck 3

B - 7850 Enghien (BELGIUM)

T. +32 (0)2 395 90 20

F. +32 (0)2 395 90 21

www.betaplus.com

betaplus@skynet.be

PHOTOGRAPHY

Jo Pauwels a.o.

GRAPHIC DESIGN

POLYDEM

Nathalie Binart

TRANSLATION

Laura Watkinson

January 2006

ISBN: 907721352X

LEFT PAGE

A *Decorvan* project.

NEXT PAGES

A *Van den Weghe* project.

CONTENTS

FOREWORD

Twenty-six inspiring projects created by leading architects and interior specialists are introduced here under the title of *CLASSICAL LIVING*.

This is a label that can be applied to many different homes: houses in the countryside, built with reclaimed materials, painstakingly restored farmhouses, grand town houses, a minimally designed villa where antiques and design go hand in hand, a house by the sea, furnished in a contemporary classic style,... the list goes on.

In spite of the significant differences between the projects presented in this book, there are some themes that keep recurring: the consistent choice of quality products, the respect for traditional craftsmanship and individually customised work and the sophisticated use of colours, textures and materials in a serene and pleasant living environment.

Without a touch of nostalgia, all of these reports show the harmonious association and integration of elements of the present and the past to form a new, contemporary whole.

Wim Pauwels
Publisher

LEFT PAGE

A project by *Devaere* in a
restored villa by the sea.

NEXT PAGES

The interior of this restored
town house in Antwerp was
created by *Decorvan*.

PART I

COUNTRY LIVING

TRENDSETTING STYLE IN THE ANTWERP KEMPEN

This charming Kempen country house, situated along a lane of beautiful plane trees in the green outskirts of Antwerp, was built by *Vlassak-Verhulst* and furnished by *De Vos Projects*.

It is one of eight rural homes in an area of parkland devised by the ambitious design team from *Vlassak-Verhulst*. The house has its own character, but still fits in perfectly with the seven other houses that have been constructed here in a typical Kempen style.

This Kempen country house was built from old "paepesteen" bricks and reclaimed red Boom tiles. The thatched part of the roof has been laid irregularly, in the traditional style. Part of the façade has been rendered with lime and has virginia creeper growing up it. Garden paving in old Dutch clay clinker bricks.

The orangery offers a beautiful garden view. The terrace is made of antique bluestone slabs. The outside sitting room is a design by *Piet Boon*.

Striking features are the typical Kempen divided-light windows with solid sills and lintels in Belgian bluestone, and the dormer windows, the sides of which have been finished with old, small slates.

P. 20-21
With her use of solid materials, *Christel De Vos* has created a minimal look that contrasts with the classic architecture of the outside of the building. The kitchen was created by *Obumex*; furniture and window treatment in collaboration with *Sphere*.

A REAL LONG ISLAND ATMOSPHERE

This house, inspired by the architecture of Long Island (the "Gold Coast" of the United States), was built by the respected villa-construction company *Vlassak-Verhulst*.

The walls were panelled with solid wood throughout and painted white. The dark oak-wood floor has been burnt and oiled. A mantelpiece covered with sterling leaf silver. White wooden inner shutters have been used instead of curtains.

LEFT
The spacious kitchen has been given a dark-tinted wooden floor and tiled with original zeliges.

DOWN BELOW
The house is rich in fascinating details, such as a frontage with a typical American porch, reclaimed machine-cut stone, staggered roofs, grey-beige painted-plank exterior walls and white sash windows. The front garden has been planted with box and yew. An authentic American panelled door with a fanlight allows a perfect ingress of light into the hallway.

LEFT PAGE
The walls in the dining room have been painted blue using a stripe technique. A dark oak floor.

A DISTINCTIVE NEW VILLA
IN WOODED SURROUNDINGS

This exclusive villa, situated in wooded surroundings, was recently constructed by the respected building contractor *Belim Bouwteam* to a design by architect *Dirk Van Vlierberghe*.
The idyllic setting represented a particular challenge: to build a house that would suit the location.

Partly thanks to the good relationship with the owners and the significant creative contribution made by the lady of the house, the result is a home that fits in perfectly with the owners' way of life. An ideal mix of old and new elements, of authenticity and cosiness, in a contemporary living environment.

The exterior architecture consists of two parts: a tall, monumental building (which includes the living room) and the side-buildings.
The main building is built in broken bond with hand-formed bricks that have later been rendered with lime.
The roof is tiled with natural slates, toning down the formal character of the house.
The side-buildings are constructed of reclaimed "paepesteen" bricks, laid in cross bond. The old red Boom tiles are a reference to traditional farmyard barns. The entrance hall is located in a protruding section of the house with a French roof. All of the windows have been painted in a mouse-grey colour. Gates and doors are made of oak.

P. 28-31

The supports of the arches on the covered terrace
are made of aged bluestone.

P. 33-35
In the library and the sitting room, the aged-oak plank floor links the classic and the contemporary. The austere fireplace wall is softened by the use of shades of grey on the wall.

LEFT PAGE

The interior clearly contrasts with the classic exterior of this villa: contemporary simplicity, but with a warm colour palette.

The grey natural-stone floor in the hall is in Azul Castilla.

The lights above the dining table create the atmosphere in this living space.

The kitchen is made up of stainless-steel and ebony units.

A wall separates the bedroom
from the dressing room, which
opens onto the corridor.

LEFT PAGE AND ABOVE
The stone-clad shower
room is separated from
the rest of the bathroom
by a glass wall.

The children's bathrooms are unusual
because of the tiled container effect
used to separate the wet rooms
(including the shower) from the
parquet floor.

ATMOSPHERE AND ANTIQUES
IN A NEW HOUSE IN THE COUNTRY

This classic country house, designed by architect *Dirk Van Vlierberghe*, has been furnished in a particularly subdued style by *Brigitte & Alain Garnier*, a married couple who are both antiques dealers.

Francis Van Damme, kitchen builders *De Menagerie*, *Descamps Decoratie* and *La Campagne* also played a role in ensuring the success of this project.

The garden is a design by *Willem Burssens*.

The sofa was specially made by *Garnier* (model: "Poly"). The coffee table with its old elm surface and wrought-iron base was also supplied by *Garnier*.

The table, the lamp and the painting come from *La Campagne*. The colourful eighteenth-century carpet was selected by *Brigitte & Alain Garnier*.

Two nineteenth-century walnut chairs around a German table (also walnut) with a Chinese lamp, all by *Garnier*.

An old vineyard table with an "os de mouton" armchair and a Louis XIII chair, both from the seventeenth century.

The banquette was found at *La Campagne*.

The 18th-century Dutch oak display cabinet has been patinated by *Garnier*.

The round dining table on one central leg was made by the *Garnier* workshops and is available made to measure. Ten nineteenth-century chairs and, to the left, a walnut console with original red marble, all by *Garnier*.

This dining area, furnished with antiques
from *La Campagne* and a *Garnier* chair
and footstool, fits in with the kitchen.

The kitchen was built by
De Menagerie to a design
by *Francis Van Damme*.

The wine cellar was
also designed by
Francis Van Damme.

The bedroom and bathroom were created by *Descamps Decoratie*.

PART II

CITY HOUSES

SYMBIOSIS OF OLD AND NEW
IN A 16TH-CENTURY LISTED BUILDING

Bart Pycke, Pascale Broos, Dimitri Bratkowski and *Stijn De Cock* purchased a dilapidated listed building, built in 1571, on the old wharfs of the Scheldt in Antwerp for the new offices of *Themenos*, their architectural firm.

With a great deal of respect for the few original details, the house was renovated and, primarily, restored to the way it once was. A number of old prints and paintings of the old town centre were at the basis of the first sketches for the design of the frontage and the internal layout.

The impression of calm and luxury that you feel when you walk through this medieval house bears witness to the pure and classic shape of the designs that it is based on.

The building, which has been completely restored to its former glory, now also houses their *La Garnerie* showroom.

The *Themenos* architects are striving for a synthesis of apparently incompatible forms from the Middle Ages and classic minimalism by placing the furniture from the *La Garnerie* collection in this 16th-century house.

The ice-blue upholstered *La Garnerie Corianders* invite you to take a rest in front of the whitewashed fireplace. Only the small wrought-iron window provides light in the adjacent room.

NEXT PAGES
The modern glassware picks up subtly on the colour of the armchair. The spaces are interwoven.

LEFT PAGE

Only a thin basket arch separates the herenkamer (gentlemen's room) from this room overlooking the square, a haven for four-thousand-year-old Afghan implements from the Daktris culture.

The misty green of the photo piece as an ideal contrast for the purple profusion of the furniture from the *La Garnerie* collection, with the old oak ceilings and floors as neutral support.

LEFT PAGE

The light is captured in large fabric shades, supported by halogen spots. Chairs with covers of different colours around a bamboo dining table.

The subtle combinations of colours and materials ensure a symbiosis of old and new. The grey ash shades of the fabrics interweave with the parallel shades of the floor and the fireplace.

LEFT PAGE
The flames of the enormous medieval Burgundy fireplace are reflected in the old polished church floor. Some antique jade rings as a symbol of infinity have been used to decorate the room.

The old shapes of the sofas were chosen for their contrast with the simple greige upholstery. On the coffee table are three antique Chinese vases. All of the shades can be found in the hand-tufted cotton, wool and flax carpet.

Movable poufs can easily be pulled up to sit on, or serve as decorative objects.

Left page

A work area in a living space.

METAMORPHOSIS OF AN OLD COACH HOUSE

This coach house, dating from the end of the nineteenth century and situated in south Antwerp, has been restored in an authentic way by interior architect *Ariane von Rothkirch* and adapted to modern requirements for comfort.

She used natural materials (such as wood, stone, marble and lime paints) with the intention of creating a contemporary home in an historic setting.

The whole rear wall has been rendered in greige lime to counter the porosity of the old pointing. All of the ground-floor windows have been replaced by French windows based on an old model.

The terrace, made of reclaimed bluestone slabs, lies alongside a box garden.

The entrance hall has been kept intact and painstakingly restored by *Ariane von Rothkirch*. The walls have been painted with specially blended lime paint. Halogen spots have been installed in the wall along the stairs.

The existing panels in the large salon have been scoured.
The mantelpiece is made from an unusual blue Burgundy
stone from Beaune.
An old oak surface from a dining table has been converted
to make a coffee table.
Above the fireplace is a work by *Leraille*.

P. 78-79
The authentic 18th-century marble fireplace and the
oak shelving are new additions to the room. Above
the mantelpiece is an antique Turkish cartwheel;
above the radiator is a display of roof-truss models.

LEFT PAGE AND ABOVE

The existing "marmoletto veneziano" kitchen
floor has been restored.

The new kitchen with its *Lacanche* stove is made
from rough, untreated oak, finished with work
surfaces and a reclaimed bluestone washbasin.

LEFT

A view through to the bathroom
with an English secretaire in the
foreground.

RIGHT

The upstairs corridor. To the right, a mahogany
console with a collection of wool winders. To the
left, the original built-in linen cupboards.

LEFT PAGE

A linen-covered *chaise longue* and an eighteenth-century
German *marqueterie* chest. Smoked oak plank floor.
Walls and ceilings in lime paint.

NEXT PAGES

The main bedroom with an antique English
rafraîchissoir at the foot of the bed.
Above the chest of drawers is a French
tapestry cartoon.

An antique patinated Swedish secretaire.

Two old food troughs have been transformed into washbasins. Above are mirrors with driftwood frames. Wooden floor in smoked oak. The shower is clad with bluestone.

Above the chest of drawers is a collection of swords and other weapons.

NEXT PAGES
The oak of the bed
and the chair has been
treated with lye.

The main bathroom, finished in
Arabescato marble, which has been
installed in an open-book pattern in
the shower. Taps by *Volevatch*.

PART III

INSPIRING PROJECTS

A FASCINATING MIX OF CLASSIC AND CONTEMPORARY IN A RESTORED PRESBYTERY

An old presbytery from 1765 and its surrounding garden had become completely neglected by the end of the 1990s.

This historic house has been restored in an authentic way, and a very contemporary kitchen extension, designed by *Robbrecht & Daem Architects*, has been added.

The garden has been redesigned to plans by landscape architect *Erik Dhont*.

Interior architect *Nathalie Van Reeth* has created a timeless whole that does not harm the historic character of the existing house.

The modern kitchen extension, designed by *Robbrecht & Daem Architects*.

The original floor, the old ceiling mouldings and the doors on pivots have been restored.

This room has been fitted out as a cloakroom, with a large oak wall that has a lavatory and coat cupboard behind it.

Washbasin in bluestone, with an old brass garden tap.

The mouldings and the mantelpiece show that this room has previously been renovated. The Dienst Monumentenzorg (department for the preservation of monuments) asked for these elements to be left intact.
A large custom-made sofa covered in an aged velvet material. The natural linen carpet was woven specially for this space. Silk curtains on black rods. The custom-built shelving, the mirror, the lamp and the low table are by *Axel and Boris Vervoordt*.

The TV room has been painted in grey. The old mouldings have been retained here as well, but the mantelpiece is new (required by Monumentenzorg). The custom-built sofa is covered with grey linen.

The dining-room floor is made of reclaimed
church tiles. The old mouldings and doors have
been renovated. The table was specially made by
Christian Liaigre, as were the chairs and the
console. Curtains in silk and an eighteenth-century
crystal chandelier.
The large work of art is by *Michel Frère*.

LEFT PAGE AND ABOVE

The kitchen in the extension, designed by *Robbrecht & Daem Architects*.

The antique presbytery dresser in the pantry is by *Vervoordt*.

The bedroom is an oasis of calm and simplicity. The light-grey and white shades give this room a serene atmosphere. The sleeping area and the dressing room flow into each other.

MDF furniture with leather handles. The new pinewood floor has been given a dark tint. The fireplace has been restored to its original condition and simply plastered.

This room, which has been turned into a children's bathroom, has been kept in its original state, with the old mouldings and inner shutters.

Units in weathered oak, with bath surrounds in brown sandstone.

The main bathroom is English in inspiration, with an antique bath with feet. Taps and mixer by *Volevatch*.

The shower has been clad with old Italian marble. The colour of the walls reflects this grey-green marble. The inner shutters have also been retained in this room.

RENOVATION OF AN AUTHENTIC FAMILY HOME

This contemporary ground-floor home, designed in 1975 by architects *Jan Christiaens* and *Michel Marchal* in collaboration with *Top- Mouton*, has recently been renovated by *Baudouin Degryse*.

The large openings mean that the most important rooms communicate with each other and all have wonderful views to the south.
These light rooms can be closed off, if so desired, by using the sliding panels and glass doors. A study on the mezzanine looks out over the living room, giving the house a special atmosphere.

In order to preserve the authentic character of this real family home, all of the original dimensions were kept intact. The antique furniture, objects and works of art were also retained.

After thirty years, it became essential to add integrated custom-built furniture to increase the comfort levels of the house. New lighting technology has been used to create a sense of intimacy and a warmer feeling. The walls, floors and textiles have all been updated with sober, more contemporary colours and materials.

A central corridor runs through the entire length of the house, offering attractive views.
The bleached-oak parquet floors reinforce the light-filled character of this home.

Old sofas and stools by *Christian Liaigre*
covered with linen on a specially made
wool and linen carpet.
Paintings by *G. Vandenbosch*.

The guest dining room is one of the few north-facing rooms. The antique furniture harmonises with the dark mahogany decor. This room has a very intimate atmosphere in the evening.

Top-Mouton designed this very functional kitchen in 1975: a combination of formica, wood and bluestone.

This simply designed desk is made of bleached ash. Chairs by *Vitra*. Carpet in wool and linen.

The new dressing room and
bedroom in bleached ash.
The bathroom has been renovated
with wengé panelling, combined
with materials from the time when
the house was built.

A SOPHISTICATED SENSE OF COLOUR

Gert Voorjans designed the interior of this house in the Waasland countryside: an eclectic look, with surprising colour choices and a fascinating mix of contemporary and antique elements.

The classic cream-coloured hall was repainted in a typical Regency colour (Windsor green) to give more character to the central room of the house. The diptych above the door to the study is based on a painting by *Veronese*. A pair of vases from St-Paul de Vence, covered with colourful porcelain and ceramic pieces.

A Chinese jar, converted into a table lamp, on the eighteenth-century Bruges writing table.
The colourful wool carpet fits in with the colour palette of the entrance hall.

LEFT PAGE

A library table surrounded by an English armchair with sidepieces and a chair based on a traditional model and covered in a Tuscan cloth made on an 18th-century loom.

To the right of the fireplace is a large French washing tub with a beautiful bronze patina, which is used as a wood basket.

To the left is an oversized concrete standard lamp with a shade made of plaster-coated old rough linen.

An old kilim on the floor, with no pattern, but with a variety of shades.

The traditional oak parquet floor has been brought up to date with an ebony colour.

LEFT PAGE AND P. 130-131

A Biedermeier chair in the centre of the sitting room.

Above the dining table is a 19th-century Moorish-style chandelier.
The walls of the dining room are presented as blocks, painted using two colours of casein paint. On the green wall is *Martin Scholten*'s "Strumming Painter".
In the foreground is a 19th-century industrial object.

LEFT PAGE

A three-shelved curiosity unit creates a connection between the dining room and the sitting room, also making more interesting use of the passage between the two rooms. The shelves hold a collection of claret ceramic pieces, African anklets and a wooden mortar.

LIVING AMONGST ORIGINAL, HISTORIC BUILDING MATERIALS

For almost a quarter of a century, *Van Huele* has been a leading dealer in antique construction materials.

The company, based in Beernem, West Flanders (near Bruges), supplies and installs reclaimed materials at home and abroad, both for private individuals and for businesses.

Van Huele supplies everything from stock. People who are satisfied with their purchase of old bricks from *Van Huele* go on to trust the company's variety of tiles, floors, and so on, and end up having a driveway and terrace installed.

This report details a number of inspiring examples of the use of historic construction materials in recent projects by *Van Huele*.

A restored house near Ypres. Floor on the basis of the second layer of sawn original bluestone flooring, resawn in straight lines and at right angles, and polished and laid in irregular bond (*Opus Romanum*). Surfaces in old bluestone with specially made moulding.

A Heuvelland farmhouse. Old Burgundy slabs with the original patina, laid in irregular bond. Original Louis XIII white-stone fireplace with an overmantel, including the coat of arms of the previous owner and dated 1738. Ceiling specially made from original 18th-century French oak beams, with the nails removed, cleaned by hand and treated with colourless polish. An original 18th-century parquet in the raised area, laid diagonally with staggered joints. The stairs have been adapted from original old French oak elements with a matching oak balustrade.

An original Louis XV mantelpiece
in a minimal interior.

Van Huele attach a great deal of importance to the authenticity of the old construction materials in all of their projects. Basècles churchfloor in *Opus Romanum*.

LEFT PAGE
The entrance hall of a presbytery-style home. "Paepesteen" brick frame around old "papesteen" bricks laid in a herringbone pattern. The round-arched ceiling is built with the same bricks. An adapted original bluestone step.

Onder de Toren, an attractive restaurant in Hansbeke. Church floor in flagstones, selected for their rustic texture and appearance. Fitted stairs made from original Basècles steps. An original straight oak staircase.

Left, a French terracotta floor in 20x20 tiles laid in a pattern.

Right, a flagstone church floor.

Flagstone church floor.

A wooden floor with wide planks and an original pine fireplace and display counter that functions as a bar.

LEFT PAGE

Simple wrought-iron railings, fitted bluestone stairs and a wooden floor with wide planks.

Some images of antique dealer *Rik Mahieu*'s home in Damme: original 12x12 reddish brown tiles and an original Flemish ceiling, painted white (dating from 1500).

A NEW VISION ON TIMELESS LIVING

Passionate about decoration and interior design, *Flamant Home Interiors* create furniture and accessories with a timeless feel.

Paying exceptional attention to authenticity, *Flamant* work according to a concept that is simple yet strong: the use of old furniture and other items, adapted to modern requirements.

The dining room has been painted with *Gris Nuages*, a shade from the *Flamant* range of paints.

't Kasteel & 't Koetshuys is an eatery, B&B and interiors store in Veurne.

LEFT PAGE

Richard chairs (available with fixed or loose covers in all *Flamant* fabrics) around a mahogany gate-leg table.

Tablecloth from the *Autelle Collection*. Beige *Cavana* service, *Oregon Dark* cutlery and *Pinos* wine glasses. *Dennis* mirror.

A *Richard* chair and an antique desk. *Flamant* accessories.

The many authentic architectural details demonstrate the rich architectural history of this distinctive building.

The design, however, is still very contemporary. The world of *Flamant* is one of discreet luxury and intimate charm. The perfect combination of individuality, comfort and modernisation, as can be seen in this report on *'t Kasteel en 't Koetshuys*.

A mahogany *Raffles* chair with a woven seat (natural).
Edwards table, also mahogany.

This *Ducale* console with an antique white finish is also available in mahogany.
Bath products from the *Histoire d'eau* series. Towels from the *Home* series.

A wood basket with
bamboo handles. *White*
hand towels (*Home*
collection).

LEFT PAGE
The bedroom has been
painted with *Bord de
Seine* by *Flamant*.
A *Washington* pouf in
ancient green (available
with fixed and loose
covers in all *Flamant*
fabrics).
A *Duncan* bed with no
headboard and *Sarah*
bedlinen. Wall lights in a
bronze finish with a
pleated shade.

REJUVENATION TREATMENT

Architect *Bernard De Clerck* was commissioned to give a rejuvenation treatment to this twenty-five-year-old house.

Subtle alterations have given the house a new, fresh atmosphere. The open view onto the garden, originally landscaped by *André Van Wassenhove*, has been perfectly accentuated.

Seen from the hall and the sitting room, the architectural layout of the garden and the green colour palette form a beautifully composed picture.

LEFT PAGE
The wide stripes of the wall design create an effect of depth in the hallway.

New light-tinted oak doors have been installed on both sides of the fireplace wall. The wooden floor is made of dark-tinted Kambala planks.

The view of the garden gives the sitting room an extra dimension.

LEFT PAGE
In the autumn, the morning sun creates the perfect light in the sitting room. The painting by the Roeselare artist *Blomme* has been removed from its superfluous frame and hung above the grey-green eighteenth-century mantelpiece.

The washbasin, combined with a light-oak chest of drawers with a bronze bar. The wall and floor have been clad with cement tiles.

Left page
Dressing room in painted wood with dark Kambala floor. Wooden blinds soften the light.

This illuminated alcove gives the room a more abstract dimension.

LEFT PAGE

The bedroom with its dark wooden floor and a warm-tinted wall creates an exotic atmosphere.

A SOPHISTICATED SENSE OF COLOUR AND TEXTURE

This report presents three recent interior projects by *Lacra Lifestyle / Craeymeersch Project*, the trend-setting West Flemish home-furnishings store with an in-house design studio for interiors and its own workshop for window treatments and soft furnishings.

P. 162-163

A kitchen with areas for dining and cooking in a restored manor farm near Bruges. In the kitchen is a glazed-linen blind by *Dominique Kieffer*; the transparent blind in the cooking section is made of 100% linen by *Chivasso*.

A coarsely woven ecru linen from *Nobilis* has been selected for the large sitting room: a beautiful contrast with the sober grey walls. The pale wall on the right has been restored and treated with authentic patinas.

The master bedroom of a country house in Damme, with a greige taffeta material from *Dedar*, traditionally finished with heavy flannel. Bed linen by *Chris Mestdagh*.

The sitting room displays ivory accents in contrast with the black church slabs on the floor. Cotton curtain from *Nobilis*, wool and linen carpet from *Danskina* and chairs with white covers. The beams have been sandblasted and finished with an aged grey patina.

LEFT PAGE

This renovated entrance patio has been laid with old clinkers in shades of orange-brown.
The newly installed metal orangery window (previously a closed gateway) provides a connection with the natural surroundings.

The main bedroom is separated from the bathroom by a wardrobe. The door has been given an unobtrusive look. Transparent curtains in the wardrobe doors accentuate the rustic character. Curtain fabric and back panel of the bed in cotton from *Malabar*. Floor, walls and bathroom surface have been clad in brown-veined marble mosaic.

A surface in beige zelliges in this children's bathroom.

Orange accents in curtains and bed accessories (*Malabar*) in this bedroom. Bed linen by *Chris Mestdagh* and lighting by *Stéphane Davidts*.

Two impressions of *Huyze ten Hove*: subdued guestrooms in the heart of Bruges.

Wallpaper and curtain fabric by *Ralph Lauren* in the sitting room. An *Aubusson* carpet.

The wallpaper with its flower design (also by *Ralph Lauren*) creates a warm, sunny effect in the yellow room. Curtains in heavy, soft-yellow cotton.

PART IV

TRADITIONAL KNOW-HOW AND CRAFTSMANSHIP

CONTEMPORARY CLASSIC RENOVATION OF A VILLA BY THE SEA

A distinctive villa on the Belgian coast has been completely renovated by the *Devaere* interior studio, who were responsible for designing and implementing the plan and coordinating the work.

The designer of the project, *Nico Devaere*, has created a classic combination of shapes, teamed with a contemporary colour palette.

P. 174-175
The daybed offers a
unique view of the
garden and the dunes.

The panelling, which is used throughout the entire room, was painted by hand. The fireplace and mantelpiece were custom-built in solid oak by *Devaere*.

Light, subtle colour nuances in all rooms. The oak-plank floor has been treated with lye.

P. 180-181

The master bedroom.

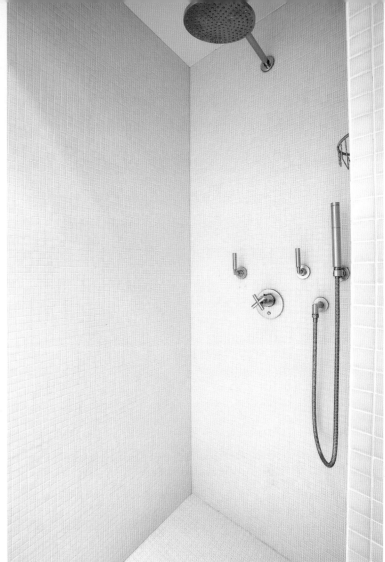

The showers have been tiled with glass mosaic and the washbasin surrounds are in Tavel Bleu stone. Washing blocks in Nero Zimbabwe granite.

Door panels inspired by the original doors, with silver-alloy handles. In the background is a work by *Roger Raveel*.

Washbasin clad with Nero Zimbabwe.

TRANSFORMATION OF AN AUTHENTIC VILLA: PAINT EFFECTS IN A STYLISH KITCHEN

Tack have made a name for themselves in recent years as leading designers and manufacturers of high-quality kitchens built in a very individual, timeless, contemporary style.

In his designs, *Frank Tack* always places the emphasis on a warm atmosphere, authentic cosiness, ease of use and comfort.

This report shows the kitchen design in a spacious, authentic villa from the 1960s, which has been transformed into a modern, light space at the request of a young, dynamic couple.

Both the dresser and the kitchen door are made of oak. The minimal design of the table fits in perfectly with the more classic look of the dresser. The glass creates a transparent effect.

LEFT PAGE

A colour accent has been placed in the ceiling, which, together with the lighting, emphasises the height of the room and creates balance. The natural light entering the space was taken into account in the choice of colours for the project as a whole. The simple lines of this design make it timeless and resistant to trends: this is possible in both classic and contemporary homes. The kitchen door is made of oak finished with lime paint to give it a velvet look.

Office, dining room and kitchen flow seamlessly into each other, but are still clearly identifiable. Whilst cooking, you still have access to the dining area.

A bar section has been integrated as a separation wall between the kitchen and the office in a way that does not interfere with the open space and the connection between the two rooms.

The chairs provide a colour contrast.

The office section has also been designed in oak with the same lime paint as in the kitchen.
The inner door was also created in the same materials.

The monochrome colour palette creates a very calming atmosphere.
As always, only high-quality materials were selected for this project.

This kitchen is the ideal meeting place for the young family to relax and calm down after a hard day at work, a real family room.

THE EXPERT KNOWLEDGE
OF A TALENTED FAMILY COMPANY

For over seventy years, *Van Overstraeten* has been a renowned firm of cabinet-makers, carrying out projects throughout the whole of Belgium.

Every project is made to measure and produced by experienced and enthusiastic experts using the best materials.

Van Overstraeten is a family company in the truest sense of the word: flexible, customer-oriented and decent.

The company has a multitude of loyal customers, including the Royal Family, who have belonged to *Van Overstraeten*'s clientele for over a quarter of a century.

Since 1995, this recognition has been crowned by the company's appointment as an officially certified purveyor to the Royal Household.

This report presents two recent total projects by *Van Overstraeten*.

The floor in the hall is made of church slabs with marble cabochons.

LEFT PAGE

This Pajottenland farmhouse has been transformed by *Van Overstraeten* into a classic country house with an atmosphere of charm and authenticity. The company coordinated everything from the design stage and the construction work to the furnishing and the finishing. The façade of the main building has been cemented and ornamental frames have been installed around the windows. The front door is based on a model from the English town of Rye.

An old stable has been transformed into an orangery. A view through the wrought-iron windows into the charming garden. The chairs, made by *Van Overstraeten*, are based on an old model.

Storage cupboards have been installed in the section beneath the window-seat.

The open kitchen has been integrated into the orangery. The work surface with its built-in sink is made of Carrara marble. Behind the soft-grey painted doors are kitchen utensils and groceries. The furniture was built in the *Van Overstraeten* workshop.

All of the appliances in the small breakfast room have been subtly integrated into the painted tulipwood furniture. The old floor with its cement tiles has been reused.

The square dining area has been furnished symmetrically with low panelling and four corner cupboards adapted to fit this space. The ceiling has been decorated with ornamental moulding.

The English-inspired bureau has been done in polished mahogany.

The radiator cupboard has been designed as a seat and gives a view of the closed kitchen garden.

The bedroom has been clad throughout in grey-painted panelling. Cupboards and two closed doors have been incorporated.

Wooden floor with wide oak planks. Painted low panelling and bookshelves.

LEFT PAGE AND ABOVE

The oak-beamed kitchen ceiling. The custom-built furniture is made from solid bleached oak with work surfaces in Belgian bluestone. A solid-oak interior door with a lock.

Painted cupboards with low panelling continuing through the room.

The cladding around the bath and the built-in linen cupboard were made by *Van Overstraeten*, as was the vanity unit with its curved doors. Surfaces in Belgian marble.

FROM LIVING KITCHENS TO TOTAL INTERIORS

Country Cooking started years ago as the exclusive importer of the legendary cast-iron *Nobel* cooking ranges.

The company later decided to develop their own kitchen line to reflect the *Country Cooking* vision, which is based on the idea that a kitchen can be furnished in just the same way as any other living space. The concept took shape: the *Doran* living kitchen was born. The right combination of furniture and colours and the integration of the appliances makes the kitchen into a pleasant and cosy living environment.

Quality comes first at *Country Cooking*: all of the furniture is made according to traditional methods in solid pine or oak. This results in kitchens with a unique atmosphere and high levels of durability. The customer can choose between a rustic atmosphere (the *CC* line) or a more minimal, contemporary look, the *LC* line.

P. 204-207

Respect for traditional principles does not conflict with the functional character of the contemporary kitchen.

Patinated pinewood in bitter chocolate and flour white from the *Doran* colour collection has been selected here, in combination with end grain and aged oak.

Country Cooking use their eye for detail to create harmonious and timeless interiors. These drying racks and sorting baskets fit in perfectly with the concept, as does the table with its solid oak top.

Doran has taken a step outside of the living kitchen and devoted attention to furnishing the complete house. Bookshelves, bathrooms, dressing rooms and, of course, separate pieces of smaller furniture have been done in the style of the house and according to the wishes of the client.

The move to total projects and individual items of furniture was an obvious one for *Doran*. As they were already working with separate solid pieces of furniture in their kitchen designs, the versatility of these individual elements was transferred to other projects.

RESPECT FOR THE CRAFT

Dirk Cousaert is fascinated by the craft of turning authentic, weathered materials into fully fitted kitchens, custom-made furniture, robust tables, bookshelves, and other such items.

His passion is a life's work, which has taken physical shape in the form of an old-fashioned furniture shop and an inspiring showroom full of old construction materials.

The three projects in this report are characteristic of the individual style of the traditional workshop of *Cousaert – Van der Donckt*.

ABOVE

Two newly installed beams support the ceiling. The oak cupboard with its wrought-iron frame harmonises with the kitchen furniture.

LEFT PAGE EN ABOVE

In this historic farmhouse in Wallonia, *Cousaert – Van der Donckt* designed a distinctive kitchen using weathered, bleached oak and wrought iron as basic materials.

The frames of the in-built refrigerator (in the background on the left) and the cooker hood are made of wrought iron, clad with robust oak planks. The work surface and the tap unit are made of aged bluestone. The washbasin is a reclaimed piece. The handles were forged by *Cousaert – Van der Donckt*.

A bridge links the parents' and the children's
bedrooms. The owner aimed to achieve the
maximum of transparency and spaciousness, so
Cousaert – Van der Donckt made a light steel
construction with steel-cord rails.

In this kitchen in a restored farmhouse, *Cousaert – Van der Donckt* went for oak with a less rustic finish.

Work surface and washbasin in bluestone.

The cooker hood is made of wrought iron. The large
amount of space makes this a very practical living and
eating space (continuation of p. 216-217).

P. 219-221

In this presbytery, built with reclaimed materials, *Cousaert – Van der Donckt* constructed bookshelves and a TV cupboard from robust French oak finished with iron posts, as well as the washbasin units in the bathrooms and the fitted kitchen.

EXCLUSIVE CUSTOM-MADE WORK: OUTDOOR KITCHENS, OUTBUILDINGS AND EXTERIOR JOINERY

Grandeur specialises in exclusive, traditionally produced joinery, oak-wood outbuildings and outside kitchens.

Grandeur outside kitchens are made according to traditional methods using robust oak with mortise joints and work surfaces in bluestone or granite.

The stainless-steel cooking unit is equipped with several burners to allow for optimal regulation of the temperature. It can be used for barbecuing, grilling, deep-frying and cooking with a wok. When the double-walled lid is closed, the unit functions as an oven. A refrigerator and other appliances can also be built in. *Grandeur* makes its outdoor kitchens to order and, if so desired, can provide a beautiful roof in the style of the home and/or garden. Show kitchens are displayed at the *Grandeur* outlet in Schoten.

Grandeur also builds cottages, covered terraces, garages, pool houses and carports using traditional methods in high-quality oak and with mortise joints.

This dynamic company also supplies unique high-quality exterior joinery for an attractive price and quality.

Grandeur provides these products for building contractors, project developers and private individuals. Installation can be carried out by the customer or by *Grandeur*.

P. 222-223

An outside kitchen in solid oak with a granite work surface, equipped with a stainless-steel gas barbecue.

These tables were specially built by *Grandeur* using traditional methods in oak with mortise joints. The lamps are turned from old oak and are available in different shapes and sizes. The wall unit is made completely of oak.

LEFT

The complete interior of this oak outbuilding was designed, built and fitted by *Grandeur*.

A 10m² garden shed with its frame and door in oak and with larchwood planks. The roof is clad with old Boom tiles.

An octagonal summerhouse in oak with a roof in old Burgundy tiles: an ornament in this beautiful English garden.

This cottage has been finished in oak throughout, with its roof clad in old Burgundy tiles.

LEFT PAGE

An outside kitchen in solid oak with a surface in Belgian bluestone, equipped with a black enamelled gas barbecue.

TIMELESS LIVING AMONGST ANTIQUES

Andreas Van Apers' business has developed over the past decades to become one of the foremost suppliers of antique construction materials in Belgium.

In recent years, this know-how has been coupled with a total vision of interior design and furnishing, particularly prompted by the initiative of the second generation of the family.

Joris Van Apers coordinated the project in this report.

A decorative detail: a 17ᵗʰ-century tapestry on the cushions.

LEFT PAGE

Old and new are harmoniously combined
in this total project by Van Apers.

ABOVE

The bookshelves were built around the original sliding doors.
Design and implementation by the Van Apers workshop.

The garden room with an aged oak-plank floor.

Detail of an old terracotta floor.

Old bluestone gateposts.

LEFT PAGE

An authentic Regency fireplace in pierre marbrière with an *Igno-For* fire system, old fireplace bricks and a surround of Burgundy slabs. Above the fireplace is an antique Italian fresco.

A BORN SPECIALIST IN PAINTS AND COLOURS

In a century and a half, the Aalst company *Schellaert* has grown from a traditional paint manufacturer to become one of the largest producers and distributors of paint in the Dender region.

Their fanatical attention to quality and first-rate customer service have been maintained over the generations.

In addition to specialising in paints, the Aalst company also offers floor coverings (rugs and fitted carpets), wall treatments and painting equipment. *Schellaert* is a real one-stop shop for the professional painter, with a large showroom and over ten thousand articles that can be supplied from stock.

This castle dating from 1870 has recently been completely renovated.

The façades have been painted and repointed using high-quality acrylic paints by *Schellaert*: a flexible, crack-sealing paint system for exterior walls.

Together with a complete team of expertly trained staff, the brothers *Jacques and Yves Mathias* are at the professional's disposal.

The centre of operations for this dynamic future-oriented vision is *Schellaert Kleurfabriek*, a paint factory that incorporates four core activities: *Schellaert Groothandel* (the distribution, storage and collection centre), the *Flamant Original Paint Collection* (producer and main distributor of this exclusive line of paints), *Pinto private label* (producer and exclusive distributor) and Novita transparent stain (producer and main distributor).

The wooden balcony of this country house on the edge of town, with its main building that dates back to 1885, has been painted with gloss *Pinto* paints from *Schellaert*.

The old caretaker's lodge (top right, p. 235) was constructed at a later date (around 1902).

The whole interior and exterior of this doctor's house have been decorated with matt acrylic paints from the *Colore di Pinto* range by *Schellaert*.

A PASSION FOR NATURAL STONE

Desloover, a specialist company from Oudenaarde, has for years been one of the most respected Belgian suppliers of tiles and natural stone.

In this home, designed by architect *Bernard De Clerck*, the company from East Flanders shows how important natural stone and tiles are in ensuring the success of a construction project.

This house is the result of a consistent determination to achieve perfect harmony between traditional construction materials and contemporary natural stone.

P. 240-243

The floor of the sitting room is laid with a Bleu de Vix natural stone in 50x70 cm tiles, done in half-brick bond.

The painstaking details of the finish contribute to the exclusive character of this large room.

In the kitchen,
traditional tiles have
been combined with
perfect custom-built
work in natural stone.

Simplicity and clean lines in the bathrooms. The washbasins and the shower walls are clad with traditionally manufactured zelliges.

The washbasins and shower walls are clad with bluestone.

Original Ortis tiles in the wine cellar.

PERFECTION IN CUSTOM-FITTED NATURAL STONE

This is a creation by *Villabouw Sels* and their interior architect *Steven Van Dooren*. All of the work in natural stone has been carried out by *Van den Weghe*.

Trompe-l'oeil effect with Massangis, Buxy Bleu and Brun in the guest lavatory.

LEFT PAGE AND ABOVE

The hall is in custom-cut French natural stone: Massangis Roche Jaune / Clair with Buxy cabochons. The staircase is also in Massangis with stone steps, some solid, some hollowed out, that perfectly follow the flow of the curving wall.

In the kitchen, aged Buxy Gris / Jaune / Cendré has been chosen, in combination with work surfaces and sinks in Bianco Statuario: a very hard white marble used by sculptors including *Michelangelo*. The area above the stove has been tiled with zeliges.

Bushhammered (anti-slip) Spanish Cenia
marble has been combined with Greek Golden
Chios in the master bathroom.

Almost pure-white Lasa marble with a smooth finish in the children's bathroom. The shower floor consists of floating slabs with open joints. The wall has been clad with marble tiles.

CRAFTSMANSHIP IN NATURAL STONE

In twenty years, *Eddy Windey* has expanded *Wiera*, his natural-stone company, to create one of the leading businesses in this sector.

Wiera Windey supplies expert natural-stone work to fit the specific requirements of individuals and professionals such as building contractors and kitchen manufacturers.

The company opened a new showroom in autumn 2005, providing a beautiful sample of the know-how of this Waas natural-stone company.

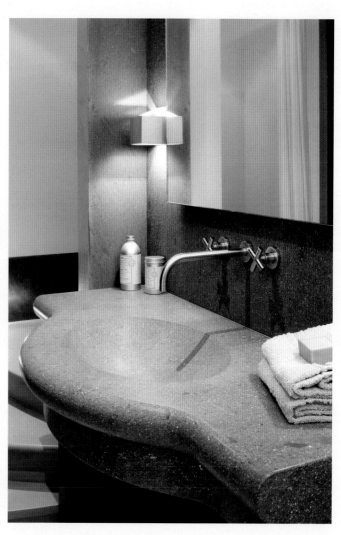

Washbasins in Pietra Piasentina (left) and Grigio Verde natural stone (right), both with a smoothed finish.

LEFT PAGE

The bath and the walls are clad in smoothed Basaltina lavastone.

Washbasin surrounds in Angola Sadinato granite.

A combination of white Carrara marble, Rouge belge and Noir de Mazy.

Combination of Chassagne natural stone and a wooden inlay.

LEFT PAGE AND ABOVE

Stairs in Chassagne beige, a French white stone.

LIVING AMONGST COLOURS:
THE AUTHENTICITY OF LIME PAINTS

Arte Constructo has made a name for itself as an international distributor of natural, mineral and environmentally-friendly products and sound construction materials such as *Unilit* (natural hydraulic lime) and *Coridecor* (fine finishing products based on lime putty), and as an importer of *Keim* silicate paints.

The *Coridecor* range consists of a variety of fine finishing products for different decorative purposes. Best results are achieved on mineral surfaces such as lime plaster, old layers of lime paint and porous stone or brick. The range offers a great deal of options, both for traditional and modern newly constructed interiors. The *Coridecor* range includes products such as lime paint (*Corical*), marble finishes (*Marmolux* and *Coristil*), Venetian stucco work (*Venestuk*) and a smooth, gloss marble finish (*Decorlux*).

Keim silicate paints can be used both inside and out, producing an even, matt finish. They are very resistant to weather and air pollution and can be applied to a wide variety of surfaces, including brick, plaster and concrete. Silicate paints are also permeable, fireproof, mould-resistant and, thanks to the use of natural pigments, colourfast.

P. 264-267

A project carried out by *Bert de Waal* using *Arte Constructo* lime paints.

As well as distributing these products, *Arte Constructo* also provides advice for architects, professionals and individuals who wish to restore an old and/or listed building in an authentic way.

This report presents three projects in which *Arte Constructo* lime paints have been used in a particularly inspiring way.

Lime paints give distinctive
buildings a unique look.
Created by *Bert de Waal*.

P. 270-275

Hand-coloured lime paints were selected for this house in the country. Created by *Dankers Decor*.